325

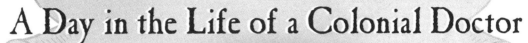

A Day in the Life of a Colonial Doctor

Laurie Krebs

The Rosen Publishing Group's
PowerKids Press™
New York

For my friend, Mary Reilly

Published in 2004 by The Rosen Publishing Group, Inc.
29 East 21st Street, New York, NY 10010

First Edition

Editor: Frances E. Ruffin
Book Design: Emily Muschinske

Photo Credits: Cover and title page, p. 4 © Independence National Historical Park; pp. 7, 11 © Custom Medical; p. 8 © Bettmann/CORBIS; p. 12 © Mary Evans Picture Library; pp. 15, 16 © National Library of Medicine/Courtesy of Pfizer Consumer Group, Pfizer Inc.; pp. 19, 20 © National Library of Medicine.

Krebs, Laurie.
A day in the life of a colonial doctor / by Laurie Krebs.
     p. cm. — (The library of living and working in colonial times)
Includes bibliographical references and index.
  ISBN 0-8239-6228-8
1. Rush, Benjamin, 1746–1813—Juvenile literature. 2. Physicians—United States—Biography—Juvenile literature.
[1. Rush, Benjamin, 1746–1813. 2. Physicians. 3. Pennsylvania—History—Colonial period, ca. 1600–1775.
4. United States—History—Colonial period, ca. 1600–1775.] I. Title. II. Series.
  R154.R9 K74 2003
  610'.92—dc21
                                                                    2002000098
Manufactured in the United States of America

Dr. Benjamin Rush was a physician who lived in Philadelphia during the eighteenth century. He was a patriot, a surgeon general to the Continental army, a signer of the Declaration of Independence, and a U.S. treasurer. Dr. Rush's responsibilities as they appear in this book are factual, but the details describing those responsibilities are fictionalized.

Contents

Benjamin Rush, Physician

Shortly before noon on a spring day in 1788, a carriage stopped near a house facing one of Philadelphia's cobblestone streets. A middle-aged gentleman climbed down from the carriage. He tied his horse to a post and reached inside the carriage for a wooden medicine chest. The man was Dr. Benjamin Rush. He was a well-known doctor making his first house call of the day.

Inside the chest were the dried **herbs** and other remedies, or medicines, that a colonial doctor might use to treat his patients.

◀ *Benjamin Rush was a signer of the Declaration of Independence.*

A Sense of Humors

Ancient Greeks believed that good health depended on a balance of the body's **fluids**, called humors. Early doctors believed that removing some of a patient's blood and other fluids would help to cure a person who was ill. In the eighteenth century, physicians, including Benjamin Rush, still believed it. This morning, he found Widow Carter flushed with a fever. Believing her fluids to be out of balance, Dr. Rush drew blood from her veins. He did not know that bleeding weakens patients and often makes them sicker.

These instruments were used for drawing blood in colonial times. ▶

Becoming a Doctor

There were few medical schools in colonial America. Most young men became **apprentices**, studying with older doctors until they could open their own medical **practices**. When Benjamin Rush graduated from college, he became an apprentice of Dr. John Redmond of Philadelphia. In 1766, when he was 20, he traveled to Edinburgh, Scotland, to study medicine. Doctors from many countries studied there. He returned home to set up a medical practice, and taught students at the College of Philadelphia.

◀ *This is an 1892 photograph of Edinburgh College Hospital.*

Dreaded Diseases

In colonial America no one knew about germs or worried about cleanliness. **Superstitious** people thought evil spirits caused illness. Religious people believed sickness was a punishment from God. Others thought "bad air" caused disease. Some people believed that bathing would make them ill. Terrible **epidemics** swept through cities and towns. Dr. Rush and other colonial doctors did not know that many of these diseases were **contagious**. Their old-fashioned treatment methods failed, and many people died.

In the late 1700s, people were first vaccinated to prevent smallpox. ▶

Accidents, Surgery, and Infection

Accidents were also common in Dr. Rush's day. Doctors had to stitch cuts, treat wounds, and set broken bones. Sometimes a doctor had to amputate, or cut off, a badly injured arm or leg. There was no **anesthesia**. Patients had to bear the pain during the operation. The worst part was that nothing was very clean, not the instruments used during the operation, the bandages, or even the doctor's hands. Often patients who survived an operation died afterward from infection.

◀ *Surgery performed in colonial times was very painful for the patient.*

The Apothecary

Dr. Rush entered the apothecary shop, or colonial drugstore. He sniffed the air with pleasure. Bottles of liquids lined the shelves. Powders and packets of pills were stacked on a counter. Herbs and roots used in medicines were heaped in two separate bins, one for preventing illnesses, the other for curing illnesses. From a jar of leeches, or blood-sucking worms, he selected several fat ones. If Widow Carter still had her fever, he would use them to bleed her tomorrow. Dr. Rush paid for the leeches and left the shop.

This is an image of a 1729 apothecary shop. ▶

Colonial Remedies

From the beginning of time, people from one generation to another have passed down remedies that they believed would cure illness. Some remedies were useful. Most were based on superstition. Many were just plain strange, such as holding a freshly-killed chicken against a patient's bare feet to cure the flu. One useful remedy came from Native Americans. They taught colonists to chew the inner bark of a willow tree to ease their aches and pains. It worked. The same **ingredient** is now found in the aspirin that people use today.

◀ *This is a re-creation of the first hospital pharmacy in America.*

Benjamin Rush, Patriot and Army Surgeon

Dr. Benjamin Rush was a true patriot. As a **delegate** to the **Continental Congress**, he had signed the Declaration of Independence in 1777. He had fought in the **American Revolution**, and had been made the army's surgeon general. By midafternoon of his busy day, Dr. Rush visited his friend Joshua Martin, a former army officer who was injured in the war. After treating wounded soldiers on the battlefield, Dr. Rush saw a connection between cleanliness and good health.

This log cabin is a re-creation of a Revolutionary War hospital hut. ▶

Instituted April 12, 1786.

A New Look at Things

Benjamin Rush was admired both as a doctor and as a teacher. He developed and used many new ideas for treating patients. In 1786, he had founded the Philadelphia Dispensary, the first place in America to give medical care to the poor. He worked there for years without pay. On this busy day in 1788, he stopped at Pennsylvania Hospital to check on the mentally ill patients. Unlike others in the 1700s, Dr. Rush believed these people should be treated with kindness, instead of being punished like criminals.

◀ *This is a wood engraving of the Philadelphia Dispensary.*

Benjamin Rush, Humanitarian

Dr. Rush was a humanitarian, which means he worked to improve the well-being of people in other areas besides medicine. He helped to organize the first antislavery society in America. He favored free public schools and the education of women. He protested against **capital punishment**. Daylight was fading when Benjamin Rush drove his carriage into the barn to unhitch his horse. Now, at day's end, like other men, he was simply coming home. His wife, Julia, was expecting him, and he was eager to see his children.

Glossary

American Revolution (uh-MER-uh-ken reh-vuh-LOO-shun) Battles that colonial soldiers fought from 1775 to 1783 to win independence from England.

anesthesia (an-us-THEE-zhuh) Medicine that relieves pain.

apprentices (uh-PREN-tis-ez) Young people who learn a skill or trade.

capital punishment (KA-pih-tul PUH-nish-ment) To put someone to death for a crime.

contagious (kun-TAY-jus) Something that is easily spread from one person to another.

Continental Congress (kon-tin-EN-tul KON-gres) The group of men who governed America during colonial times.

delegate (DEH-lih-get) A person who presents ideas on behalf of many people.

epidemics (eh-pih-DEM-iks) The quick spread of diseases so that many people have them at the same time.

fluids (FLOO-idz) Liquids.

herbs (ERBZ) Plants used for medicine or for seasoning food.

practices (PRAK-tis-ez) Doctors' businesses.

ingredient (in-GREE-dee-int) One part of a mixture.

superstitious (soo-per-STIH-shus) To believe in something that cannot be logically explained.

Index

Primary Sources

Cover: Portrait of Dr. Benjamin Rush. From Independence National Historical Park. **Page 4:** Oil painting of Dr. Benjamin Rush by Charles Willson Peale. **Page 7:** Photograph of instruments used for collecting blood; (inset): Doctor collecting blood from a patient. Artwork by English caricaturist James Gillray (1804). **Page 8:** Photograph of Edinburgh College Hospital (1892). **Page 11:** Edward Jenner administering smallpox vaccine in the eighteenth century. Photogravure of a painting by Georges-Gaston Melingue. **Page 12:** Engraving entitled The Death of [Dr. Samuel] Johnson. From the Mary Evans Picture Library. **Page 15:** The Marshall Apothecary (1729–1825). Photomechanical reproduction. **Page 16:** America's first hospital pharmacy (c. 1775). Photomechanical reproduction of Pennsylvania Hospital's pharmacy (Philadelphia). **Page 19:** Reproduction of General George Washington Army Hospital (1777–1778), Valley Forge, Pennsylvania. **Page 20:** Wood engraving of the exterior view of the Philadelphia Dispensary on South State Street in Philadelphia, Pennsylvania. (Founded in 1786 and demolished in 1922).

Web Sites

Due to the changing nature of Internet links, PowerKids Press has developed an online list of Web sites related to the subject of this book. This site is updated regularly. Please use this link to access the list:

www.powerkidslinks.com/llwct/dlcdr/